1. The rugged Haena coastline in the afternoon sun.

2. "Bali Hai" beach where the movie, "South Pacific", was filmed.

4. All of Hanalei Bay.

5. The Hanalei Valley, River, and taro from the roadside lookout.

6. Hanalei Bay from Princeville.

8. Golf at Princeville.

9. Kilauea Lighthouse during storm surf conditions.

10. The boat to Fern Grotto on the Wailua River.

11. Wailua River meets the sea near Coco Palms.

12. The Fern Grotto of Wailua.

13. Tropical exotics.

14. Wailua Falls from the air.

15. Coconut Plantation at Kapaa.

17. Nawiliwili Bay, the Kauai Marriott Resort and Beach Club, and all of Lihue. Marriott Vacation Club International (800) 872-6626.

18. The USS Constitution in Nawiliwili Harbor.

19. The sand and surf of Poipu Beach.

21. Poipu Beach, Park, and neighborhood.

22. Spouting Horn.

23. Waimea Canyon – erosion at the wettest spot on earth.

25. Kalalau Valley from the lookout at Kokee.

26. Sunset over Niihau from Kauai.

27. Napali's rugged cliffs.

29. The beach at Kalalau Valley.

30. The magic of the Napali Coast from a Zodiac.

31. Sky, beach, waters, and cliffs – the colors of Napali.